The Life and Work of...

# CLAUDE MONET

Sean Connolly

**Heinemann**
LIBRARY

# www.heinemann.co.uk

Visit our website to find out more information about Heinemann Library books.

To order:

☎ Phone 44 (0) 1865 888066

🖷 Send a fax to 44 (0) 1865 314091

💻 Visit the Heinemann Bookshop at www.heinemann.co.uk to browse our catalogue and order online.

First published in Great Britain by Heinemann Library, Halley Court, Jordan Hill, Oxford OX2 8EJ, a division of Reed Educational and Professional Publishing Ltd. Heinemann is a registered trademark of Reed Educational and Professional Publishing Ltd.

OXFORD MELBOURNE AUCKLAND JOHANNESBURG BLANTYRE
GABORONE IBADAN PORTSMOUTH (NH) USA CHICAGO

Designed by Celia Floyd
Illustrated by Fiona Osbaldstone

Originated by Dot Grdations
Printed by South China Printing in Hong Kong/China

ISBN 0 431 13153 8 (hardback)
05 04 03 02 01
10 9 8 7 6 5 4 3 2 1

ISBN 0 431 13158 9 (paperback)
05 04 03 02 01
10 9 8 7 6 5 4 3 2 1

**British Library Cataloguing in Publication Data**

Connolly, Sean
    The life and work of Claude Monet. – (Take-off!)
    1.Monet, Claude, 1840–1926 – Juvenile literature 2.Painters – France – Biography – Juvenile literature 3.Painting, Modern – 19th century – France – Juvenile literature
    4. Painting, French – Juvenile literature 5. Impressionist artists – France – Biography – Juvenile literature
    I.Title II.Claude Monet
    759.4

**Acknowledgements**

The publishers would like to thank the following for permission to reproduce photographs: Page 4, Portrait photograph of Claude Monet in front of the pictures 'Waterlilies' in his studio. Page 5, Claude Monet 'The Waterlilies - The Clouds', Credit: The Bridgeman Art Library/Giraudon. Page 6, 'Le Havre', Credit: Bibliotheque Nationale. Page 7, Claude Monet 'The coast of Normandy viewed from Sainte-Adresse', Credit: The Fine Arts Museum of San Francisco. Page 9, Claude Monet 'Caricature of a Young Dandy with a Monocle', Credit: Giraudon. Page 11, Claude Monet 'Le Pave de Chailly', Credit: Giraudon. Page 12, National Gallery, London, Credit: Hulton Getty Page 13, Claude Monet 'The Thames below Westminster', Credit: The Bridgeman Art Library/National Gallery Page 14, Edouard Manet 'Monet in his Studio', Credit: AKG. Page 15, Claude Monet 'Boulevard St Denis, Argenteuil, in Winter', Credit: Richard Saltonstall/Museum of Fine Arts, Boston. Page 16, Boulevard des Capucines, Credit: Hulton Getty Page 17, Claude Monet 'Impression, Sunrise', Credit: Giraudon. Page 19, Claude Monet 'Entrance to the Village of Vetheuil', Credit: Exley/Rosenthal. Page 21, Claude Monet 'Haystack at Giverny', Credit: The Bridgeman Art Library/Hermitage. Page 23, Claude Monet 'The Cap of Antibes, Mistral', Credit: AKG. Page 24, Rouen Cathedral, Credit: Pix. Page 25, Claude Monet 'Rouen Cathedral, Albany Tower, Early Morning', Credit: Exley/Rosenthal. Page 26, Portrait photograph of Claude Monet and his wife Alice, St Mark's Square, Venice, Credit: Giraudon. Page 27, Claude Monet 'Palazzo de Mula, Venice', Credit: Exley/Rosenthal. Page 28, Photograph of Monet in his garden, Credit: Corbis. Page 29, Claude Monet 'Waterlilies', Credit: Giraudon.

Cover photograph reproduced with permission of the Art Archive/Musée Dorsay/Dagli Orti.

Every effort has been made to contact copyright holders of any material reproduced in this book. Any omissions will be rectified in subsequent printings if notice is given to the publishers.

# Contents

Any words appearing in the text in bold, **like this**, are explained in the Glossary.

# Who was Claude Monet?

Claude Monet, one of the most famous of the Impressionist painters.

Claude Monet was a French artist who was one of the **Impressionists**. This group of painters tried to show the change of light through the day in their paintings.

Monet painted the same **scene** many times to show the change of light.

This painting of Monet's shows clouds **reflected** in the water lily pond in his garden.

# Early years

Claude Oscar Monet was born in Paris, France on 14 November 1840. His family soon moved to the **port** of Le Havre. Claude liked being near the sea.

The port of Le Havre.

Claude was the elder son of a grocer.

Claude loved the way sunlight **reflected** off the sea. This drawing shows the coast near Le Havre.

Claude drew this when he was 24 years old.

# Schoolboy success

Claude did not like school. He made clever **caricatures** of his classmates. A local painter called Eugène Boudin saw these drawings. He wanted Claude to become a painter.

Claude drawing a young man.

Claude

Claude could pick out the important bits to draw. He was 16 years old when he made this funny drawing of a young man dressed in stylish clothes.

By the time Claude was 16 years old, he was earning pocket money by drawing caricatures.

Claude's caricature of a young man.

# Making friends

In 1861 Claude joined the army but became ill after a year. His family gave him some money to become a painter. Claude moved to Paris when he was 22 years old.

Claude and other young artists.

Claude painted this **scene** on a trip to the countryside near Paris.

Claude became close friends with other young artists in Paris. They often painted together.

What time of year do you think this picture was painted? Look at the leaves to give you a clue.

# Living in London

In 1870 Monet married Camille Doncieux. France was at war with Germany. Paris was dangerous so Monet and his wife moved to London.

This is how London looked in 1870.

The war between France and Germany in 1870 was called the Franco-Prussian War.

One of Monet's paintings of the River Thames.

Monet and his wife lived in London for a while.
Monet saw many paintings by English artists. He
painted the River Thames many times while he
was in London.

Monet admired the work of Joseph Turner.
You can find out more about him in *The Life
and Work of Joseph Turner* in this series.

# Studying light

In 1871 Monet moved to Argenteuil, a small town near Paris. He built a floating studio to study how light affects water.

Edouard Manet painted this picture of Claude Monet in his floating studio.

Monet liked to paint outside in every season. This painting shows a street in Argenteuil in the winter.

Monet painted this winter street scene in 1875.

Look at the figures in this picture. There are no clear outlines, but you can tell that they are carrying umbrellas.

# Impressionism

Monet and his friends painted quickly. Most **galleries** thought their paintings looked messy. So in 1874 the group held their own **exhibition** of their paintings.

The exhibition was held in a building in this street in Paris.

16

The exhibition was held in a photographer's studio because no art gallery in Paris would show their work!

*Impression, Sunrise*, one of the paintings shown at the exhibition.

The group became known as the **Impressionists**. The name came from the title of this painting by Monet called *Impression, Sunrise*. He had painted a harbour just after dawn.

Look carefully at this painting. There are no clear outlines at all – only an impression of a harbour just after dawn.

# Two families

Monet and his family moved in with their friend Alice Hoschede and her children. Monet now had to look after two families and eight children.

Two of the children Monet had to look after.

Monet painted this picture of the village of Vétheuil.

Monet began painting around his new home in the village of Vétheuil. He used quick **brush strokes** to show light and shape.

**19**

# Giverny

In 1879 Camille, Monet's wife, died. In 1883 Monet and the two families moved to Giverny, near Paris. He loved his new garden. He also painted in the countryside nearby.

Monet painting the countryside near his home.

Monet worked quickly. He painted the same **scenes** over and over. He wanted to show how the light could change the way a scene looked.

This picture tells us about the houses, fields and even the weather one afternoon over a hundred years ago.

# Painting trips

Monet painting a landscape.

Monet spent many months away from home each year during the 1880s. He travelled around France and painted many **landscapes**. He worked in all sorts of weather.

This picture shows the wind blowing across the seashore.

This painting shows the seashore in the south of France. Monet used quick **brush strokes**. We can almost feel the wind blowing through the trees and across the sea.

Monet hardly ever used black or brown colours in his paintings – not even to paint dark shadows!

23

# Series paintings

Monet kept painting the same **scenes** at different times. Together these pictures are known as his **series paintings**.

Rouen Cathedral, which Claude painted many times.

Claude painted Rouen Cathedral about 30 times!

Monet loved to paint the front of Rouen Cathedral. It is almost hidden by mist in this picture. Some of his other paintings show it in bright sunshine.

This painting of Monet's shows Rouen Cathedral in the early morning mist.

# Travels

Monet married Alice Hoschede in 1892. He made his last painting trips when he was over 60 years old. He went to Spain, Holland, England and Italy.

A photograph of Claude and Alice Monet in Venice, Italy.

Monet loved the buildings in Venice. They rise straight out of the water.

Monet made this painting of a beautiful palace reflected in the water.

The **reflections** are not clear like in a mirror because the water is moving.

# Water lilies

Claude spent his last years at home in Giverny. He still thought about light and shape. He died aged 86 on 5 December 1926. The other **Impressionists** had died long before that.

Monet at Giverny, where he spent the last years of his life.

Monet's love for his garden was shown by the many paintings he made of it.

Many of Monet's last works were huge paintings of water lilies in the pond in his garden. In this painting it is hard to tell where the branches above the water lilies end and their **reflections** begin.

One of Monet's paintings of the water lilies in his pond at Giverny.

# Timeline

1840      Claude Monet is born in Paris on 14 November, but soon moves to Le Havre.

1845      The artist Mary Cassatt is born in the USA.

1853      The artist Vincent van Gogh is born in Holland.

1857      Monet meets the painter Eugène Boudin.

1862      Monet moves to Paris to become a painter.

1865      American Civil War ends.

1865–66  Monet has paintings shown to the public in Paris.

1870      Monet marries Camille Doncieux and lives in London.

1870–71  War between France and Germany.

1871      Monet moves to a new house in Argenteuil.

1874      Monet helps set up the first **exhibition** by the **Impressionists**.

1876      The telephone is invented.

1879      Camille dies. The artist Paul Klee is born in Switzerland.

1883      Monet moves to Giverny.

1890      The artist Vincent van Gogh dies.

1893      Monet begins work on building a pond in the garden at Giverny.

1898      The sculptor Henry Moore is born in England.

1906      The artist Paul Cézanne dies.

1909      First public showing of Claude's waterlily paintings.

1912      Monet develops an eye illness which slows his painting.

1914–18  The First World War is fought in Europe.

1926      Claude Monet dies on 5 December.

# Glossary

**brush stroke**  mark in paint made by the movement of a paintbrush

**caricature**  funny drawing of someone

**cathedral**  large church

**dawn**  when it starts to get light in the morning

**exhibit**  display works of art

**exhibition**  a show and sale of works of art like paintings, drawings or sculptures

**gallery**  place where works of art are shown and sold

**Impressionists**  group of artists who painted outside to make colourful pictures

**landscape**  painting of the countryside

**port**  town or city on the coast where boats are sheltered

**reflect**  give a second picture of something, as with a mirror

**scene**  place or area

**series paintings**  many paintings of the same subject but painted at different times

**studio**  special room or building where an artist works

## More books to read

**What Makes a Monet a Monet?** New York: Metropolitan Museum of Art/Crabtree Books

**Changing Colour, Looking at Pictures**, Joy Richardson, Franklin Watts

**Tell me about Claude Monet**, John Malam, Evans

## More paintings by Claude Monet to see

*Poplars*, The Fitzwilliam Museum, Cambridge

*Rouen Cathedral Façade*, National Museum of Wales, Cardiff

*The Water Lily Pond*, National Gallery, London

a b c d e f g h i j k l m n o p q r s t u v w x y z

**31**

# Index